# HABITS OF A SUCCESSFUL STRING MUSICIAN

## CELLO

A Comprehensive Curriculum for Use During Fundamentals Time

CHRISTOPHER SELBY, SCOTT RUSH, AND RICH MOON

AVAILABLE EDITIONS:

VIOLIN ........................................................ G-8624
VIOLA ......................................................... G-8625
CELLO ......................................................... G-8626
BASS .......................................................... G-8627
CONDUCTOR'S EDITION .............................. G-8628

GIA Publications, Inc.
Chicago

Welcome to *Habits of a Successful String Musician*. This method book was written to help string players establish effective daily routines that ultimately lead to great music making. While practicing the various components of playing, remember that improved technique only serves to increase the *artistry* of a musical performance.

This book begins with studies on tone production, bowing, and articulation (right hand), followed by finger patterns and shifting (left hand). Subsequent studies for scales, chorales, rhythm and sight-reading make this a complete method for the advancing string musician. Each exercise has a very specific purpose that leads logically to the performance of concert music. Turn your rehearsal room or practice room into a laboratory for making music, and let your musical journey begin!

This book is divided into eight parts:



**Tips for Individual Practice:**

- Listen to a recording of your favorite artist on your instrument; then imitate that artist's sound.
- Remind yourself why you are practicing. Set goals for each practice session and devise a logical order of things to learn. Strive to cover as many Components of Playing as possible, starting with tone production (bowing variations) and then finger pattern study and scales.
- Begin practice sessions with stretching. *Stay relaxed*—tension is a performer's worst enemy.
- Practice with a mirror. Review basic technique for standing or sitting well, and use left- and right-hand calisthenics to develop relaxed, healthy positions for holding the bow and instrument well.
- Stay focused and rest five minutes for every twenty minutes of practice; unfocused practice is a waste of time and energy and is detrimental to a performer's progress.
- When practicing the sight-reading exercises in the back of the book, use a metronome and establish a slow, reasonable tempo that will allow you to play the exercises with a steady pulse.
- Record yourself and use the recording to identify personal goals for improving your skills and performance.
- Finish your practice session by playing something fun. We practice so we can improve the performance skills needed to express the musical ideas that we find so enjoyable and deeply rewarding.

---


**Habits of a Successful String Musician – Cello Edition**
Christopher Selby, Scott Rush, and Rich Moon

G-8626
ISBN: 978-1-62277-092-2

7404 S. Mason Avenue, Chicago, IL 60638
www.giamusic.com

# I Tone and Articulation

## Open String Exercises

### Even Tone - Frog to Tip

With a flawless bow hold, play the open string without counting or keeping time; pay attention to the bow's contact point, angle, weight, and speed.

### Even Bow Distribution

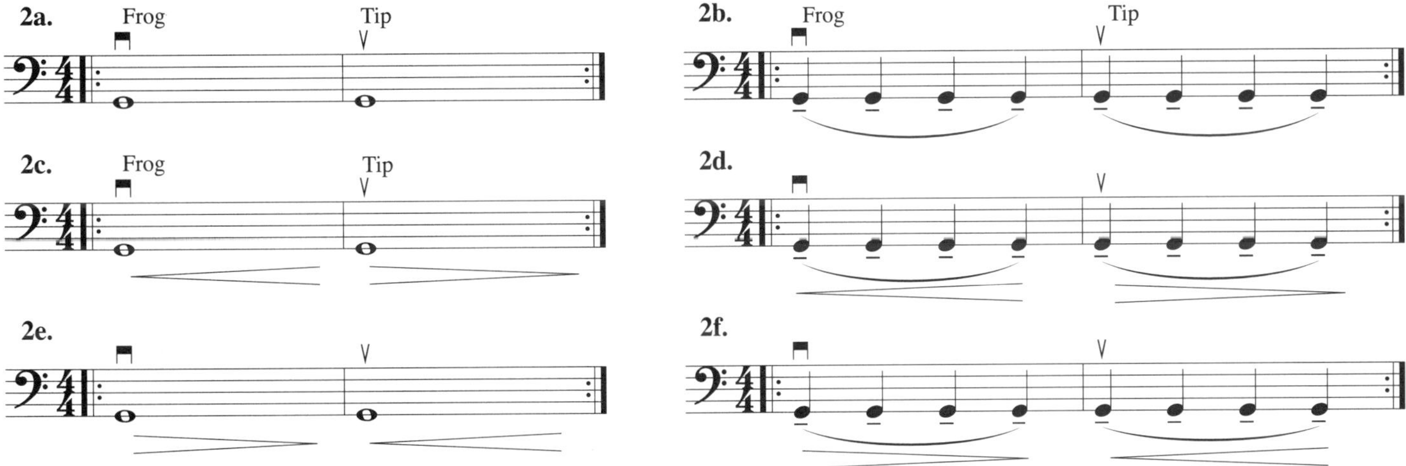


### Grab and Release

Grab the string with the hair of the bow to begin each note with a crisp attack.

### Crossing Strings

# Bowing Variations

Perform the theme using one of the rhythm or articulations from the variations below.

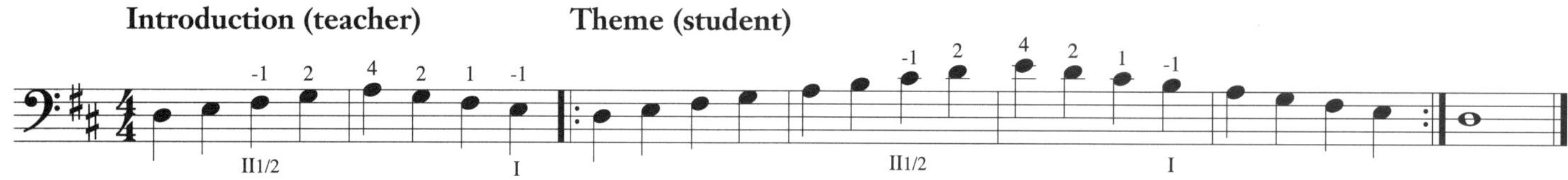


## Basic Bow Strokes

## Full Bow Exercises

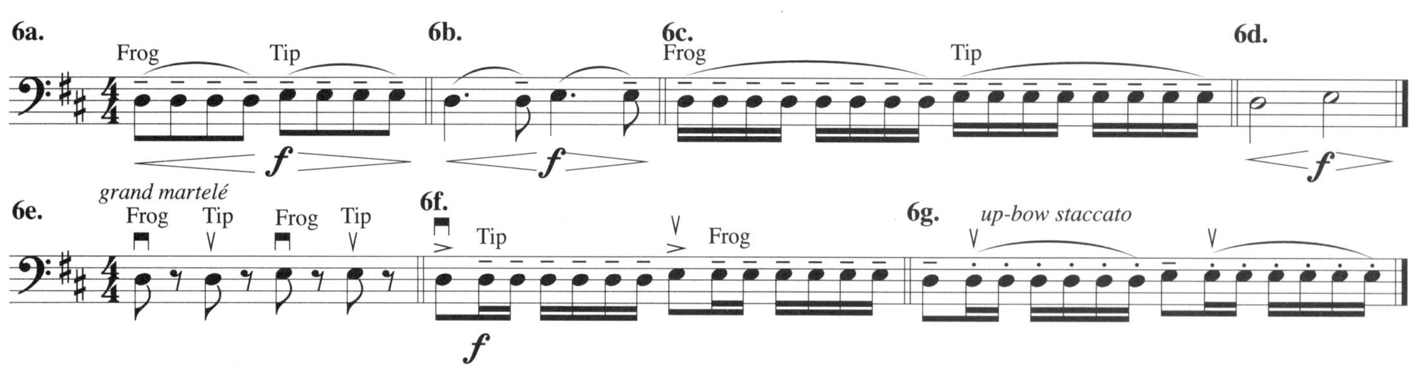


## Dotted Rhythms and Hooked Bows

## Syncopated Patterns

## Spiccato Exercises

Perform the spiccato stroke at the balance point; keep the thumb and pinky curved and the knuckles soft and fluid.

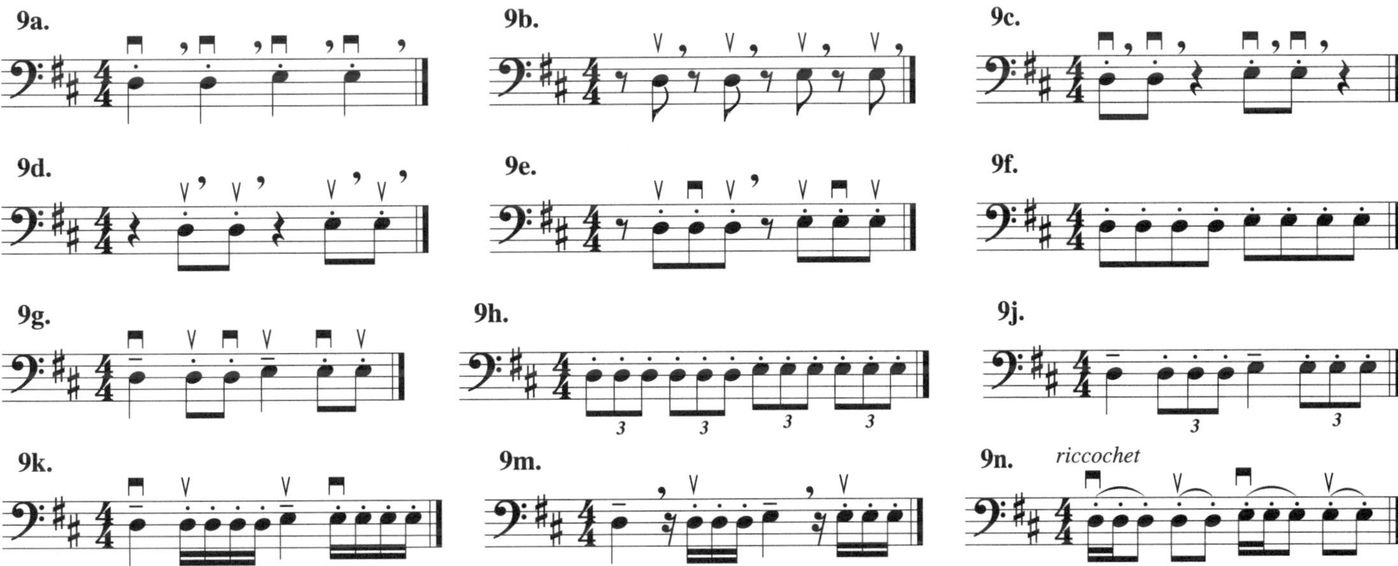


## Triple Patterns

# Slurs

# II Lower Positions: Finger Patterns, Intonation and Velocity

## 12. Natural & Sharp

## 13. Mary Had a Little Lamb



## 14. Flat Finger Pattern Exercises

## 15. Dominant Etude

## 16. Sharp Finger Pattern Exercises

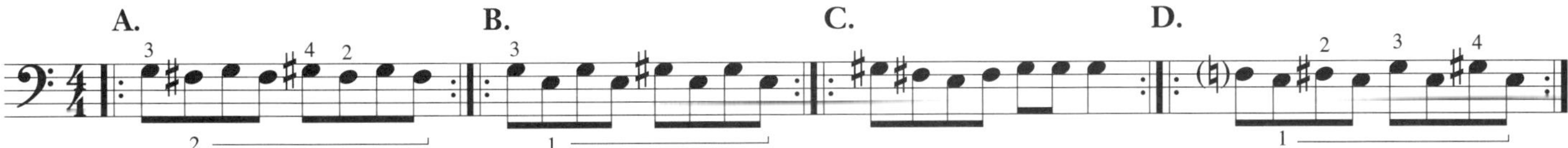


16A and B: Match the 3rd finger with open G. Keep 2nd finger perpendicular to string with the thumb directly behind it. Always keep 4th finger curved, relaxed—never stretched and straight. The extension (space) occurs between the 1st and 2nd fingers.
16C: Play all of "Mary" with the 2nd finger perpendicular to the string, and 4th finger curved and relaxed.
16D: When 2nd finger moves from F to F♯, keep it perpendicular to the string and move the thumb with it.

## 17. Changing Finger Patterns

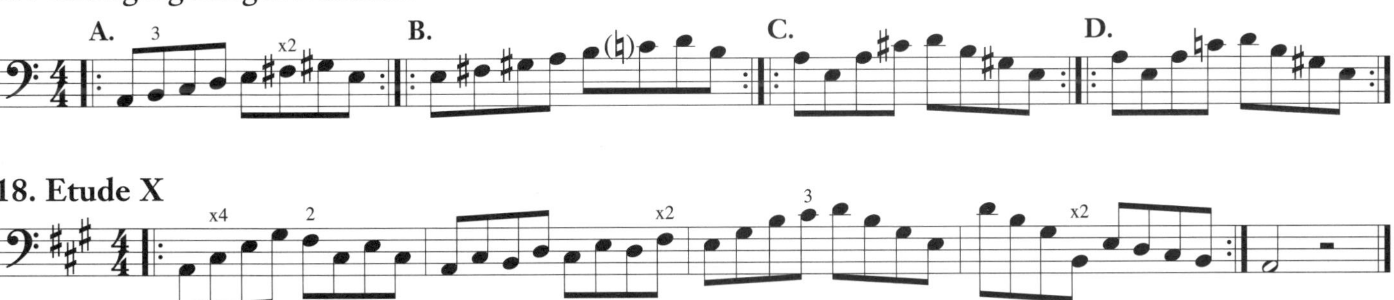


## 18. Etude X

## 19. Tetrachord Etude

Tuning Notes (Dorian Tetrachord) Etude

After learning the etude with the Dorian tetrachord above, play it with one of the other tetrachords below.

Tetrachords:

## 20. Velocity Etude

Perform the Velocity Etude as written first, and then perform it with finger pattern #2 (F♮) and #3 (E♭) shown below.

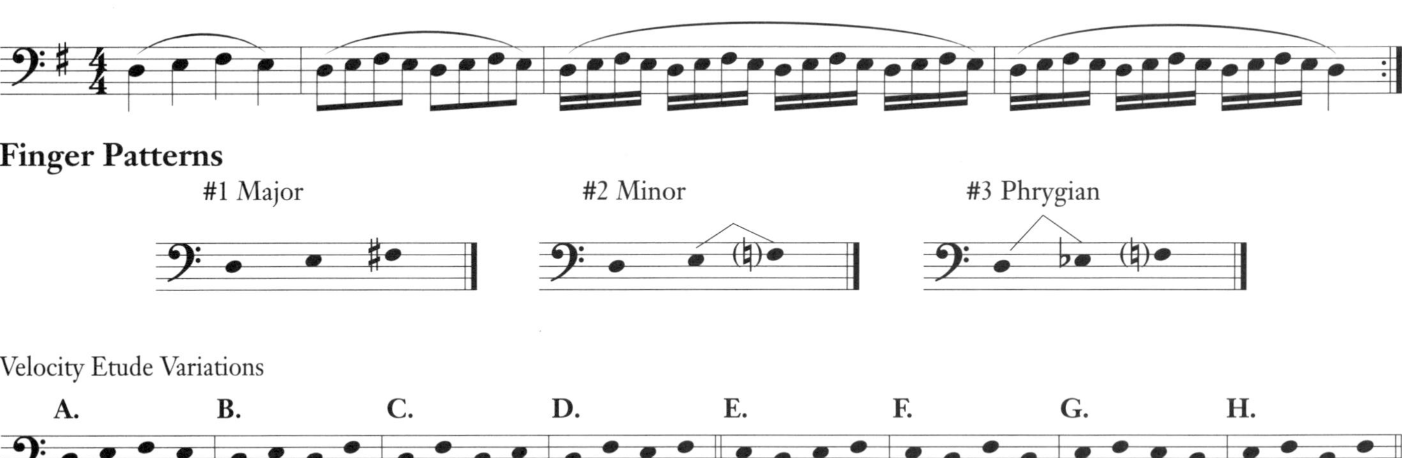


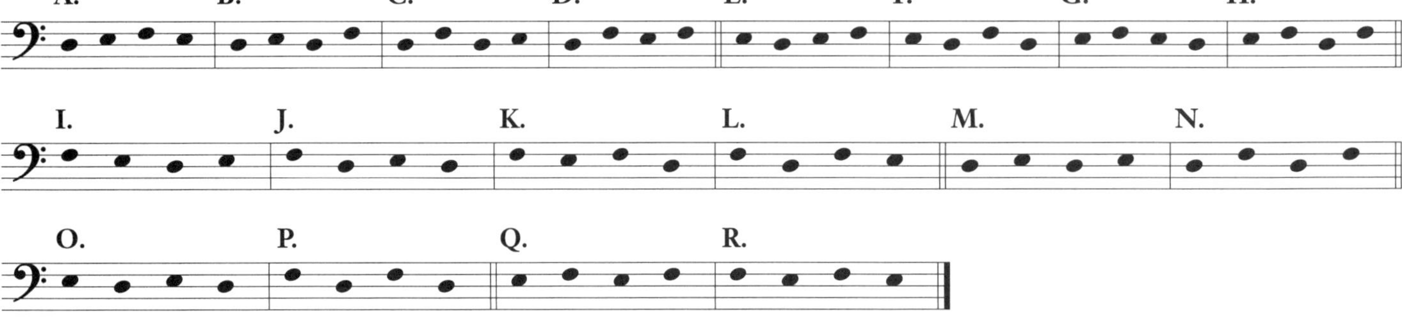


## 21. Trills

The trills on beats 2 and 4 are performed the same way.

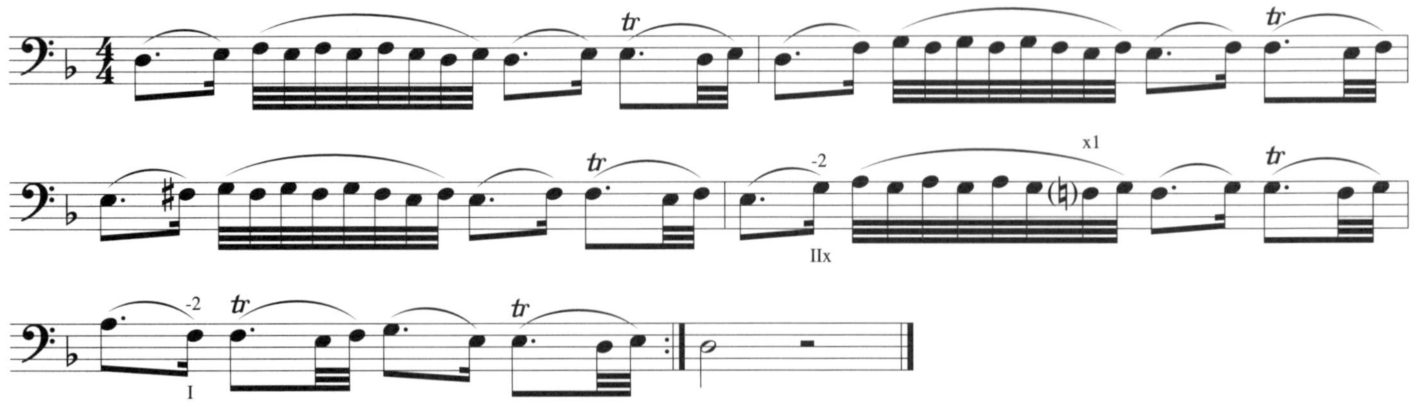

# III Shifting Exercises

Shift with a light, smooth motion; always move the thumb with the second finger.

### 22. Shifting to the Harmonic

### 23. Shifting to the Same Finger

Perform all shifting exercises with and without slurs.

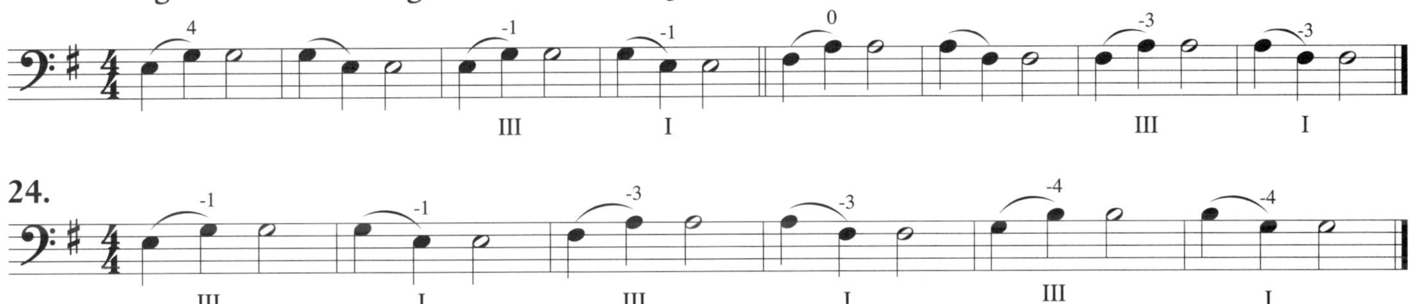


### 25. Shifting on the First Finger

### 26. Shifting to a Different Finger

♦ The diamond is the destination of the shifting finger; it is a silent shifting note that should be hidden, not heard.

27.

28.

### 29. Etude in E Minor

Mark the silent shifts with a dot or a diamond.

**30. Changing Keys** How does the key change the spacing of the shifts and finger patterns?

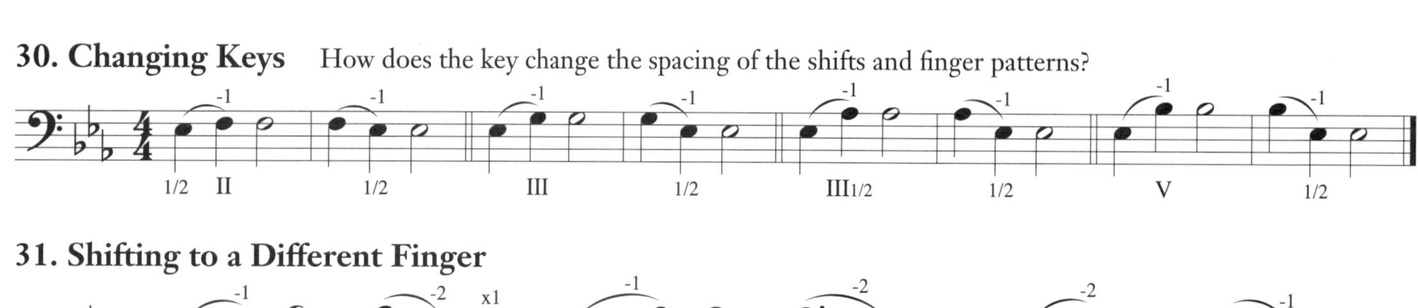

**31. Shifting to a Different Finger**

**32.**

**33.**

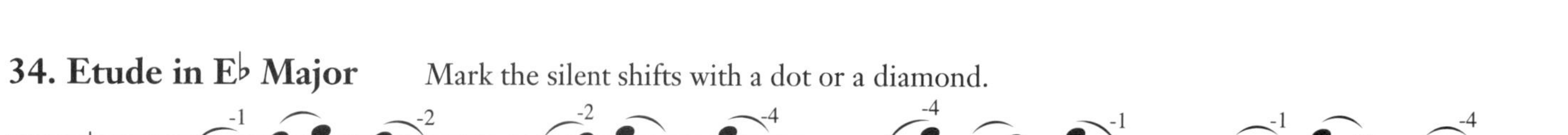

**34. Etude in E♭ Major** Mark the silent shifts with a dot or a diamond.

**35. Focus on 4th Position**

**36.**

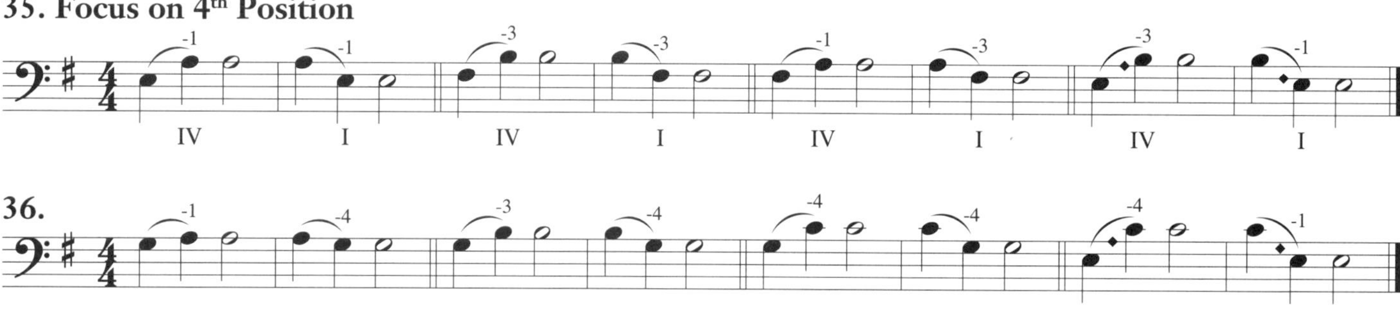

**37. Shifting to C**

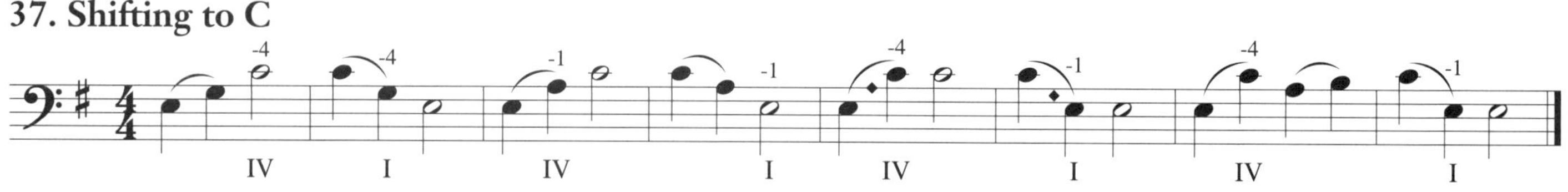

**38. Tetrachord Etude - 3rd Position**

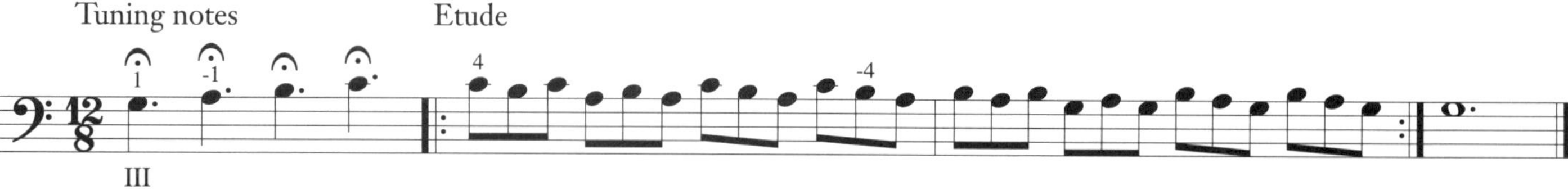


Tetrachords

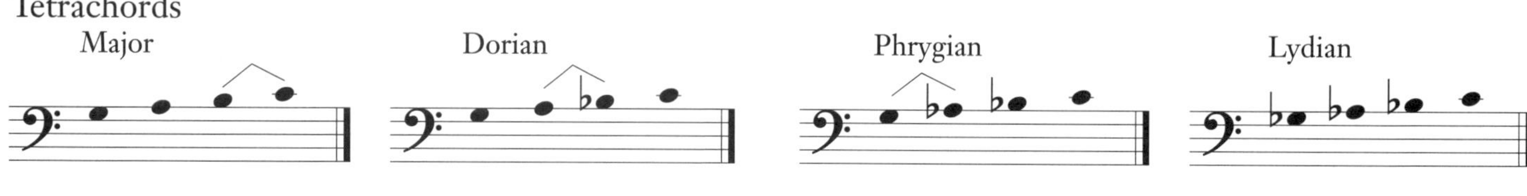

### 39. D Major Scale and Arpeggio - on One String

### 40. E♭ Major Scale and Arpeggio - on One String

### 41. Up and Down the String

To reach higher positions, bring the elbow and arm around the instrument, and the thumb around the neck.

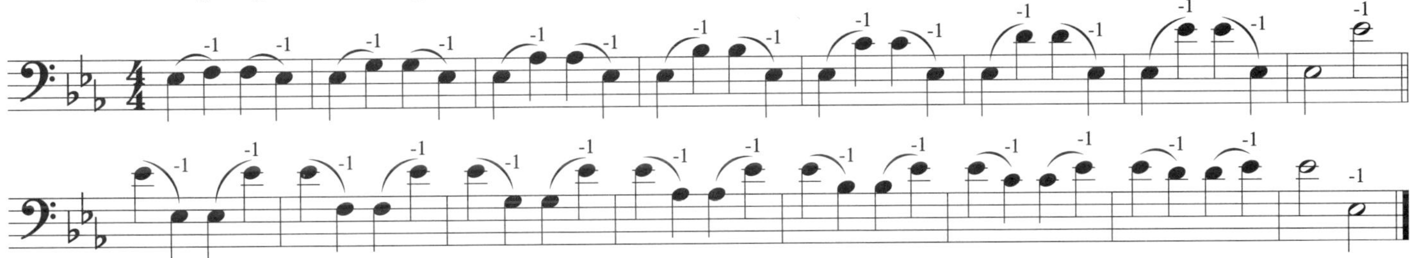

### 42. Etude in F Major

### 43. Etude in F♯ Minor

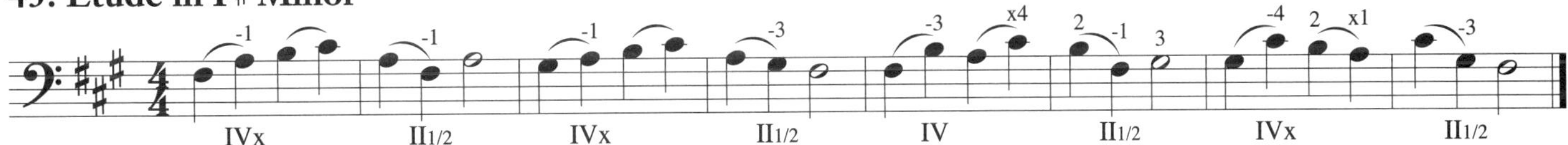

### 44. Etude in G Major

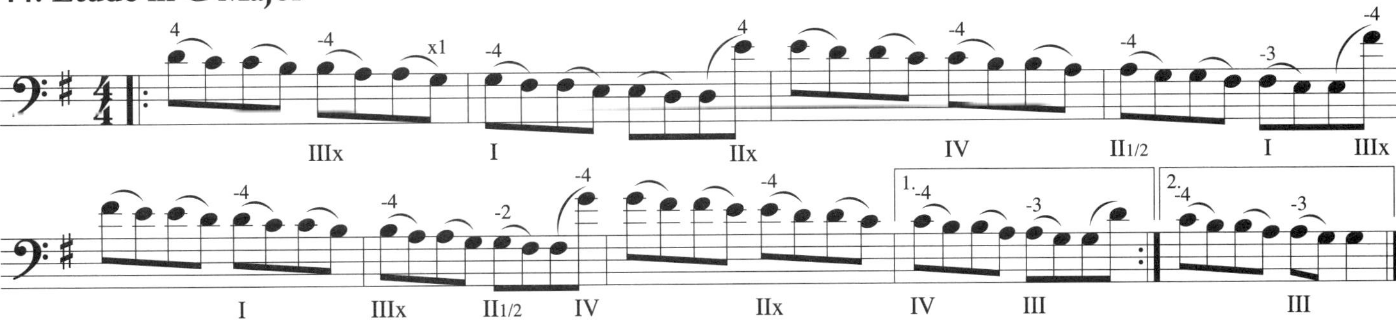

### 45. Etude in E Major

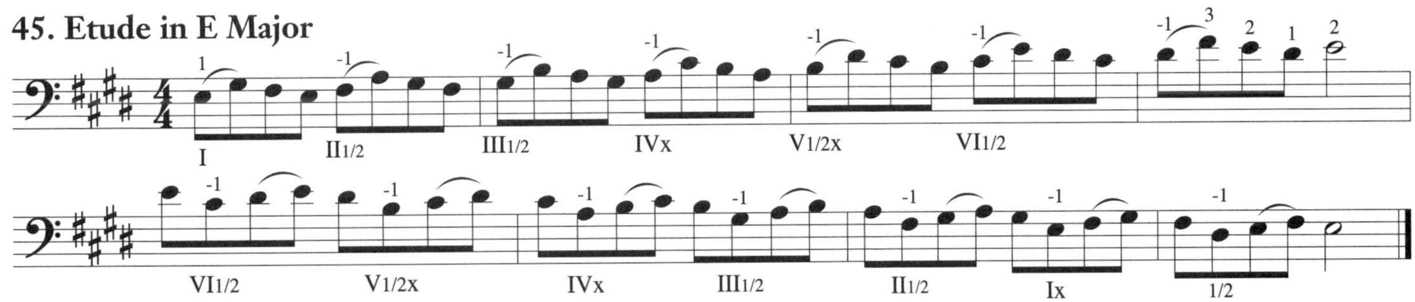

## 46. Etude in D Major

Perform as written and with three- or six-note slurs.

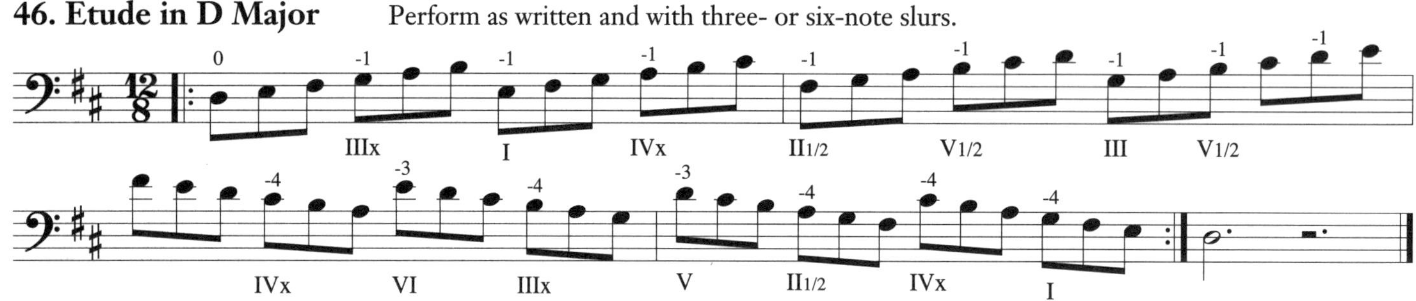


## 47. Shifty Jig

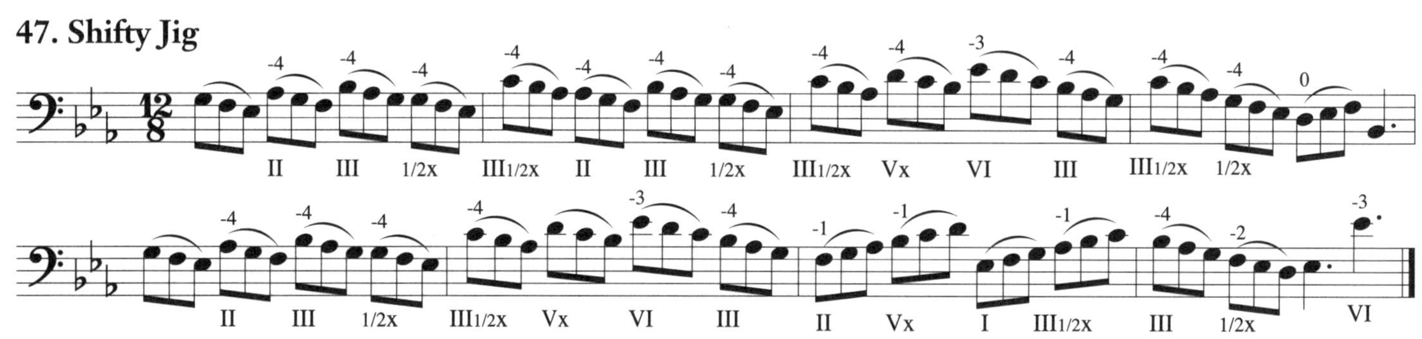

# IV Higher Positions and Alternate Clefs

### 48. Velocity Etude in Higher Positions

Perform the etude as written first, and then perform it with finger pattern #2 (F♮) and #3 (E♭) shown below.

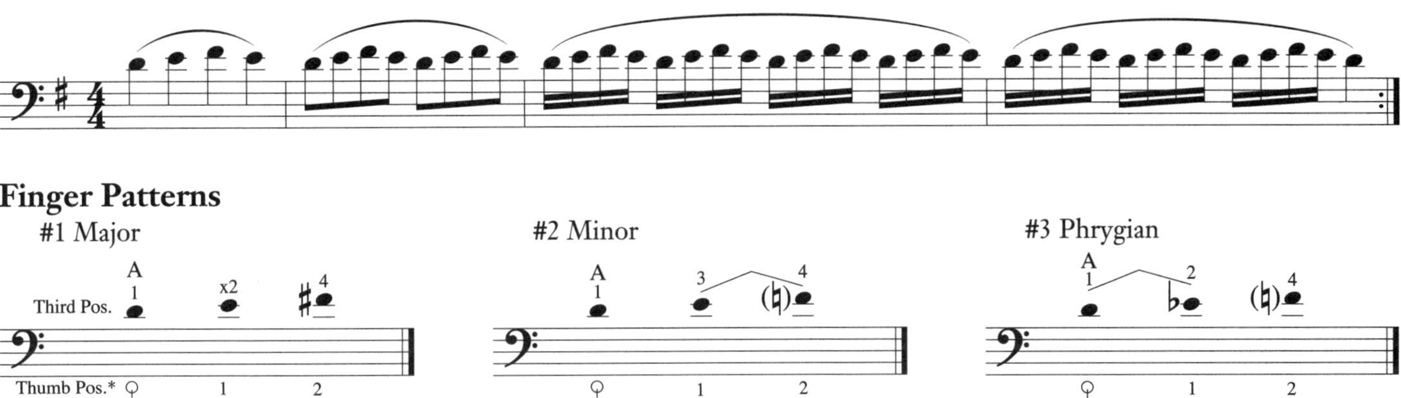


*Cello students may do the above in thumb position after learning how to play in this position on the next page.

### Velocity Etude Variations

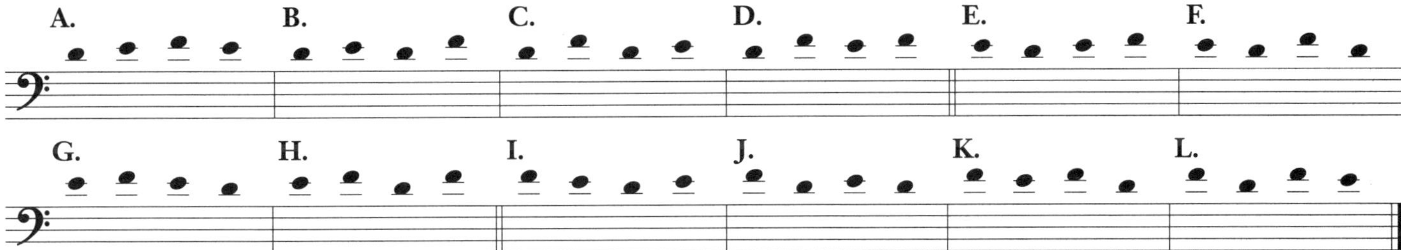


## Alternate Clefs

Violinists use ottava (8va) and lower string players use alternate clefs to reduce the number of leger lines the performer reads when the music moves into higher registers. Viola players must learn to read treble clef. Cello and double bass players must learn to read tenor and treble clefs. Advanced violinists should also learn alto clef, so they can double on viola if needed.

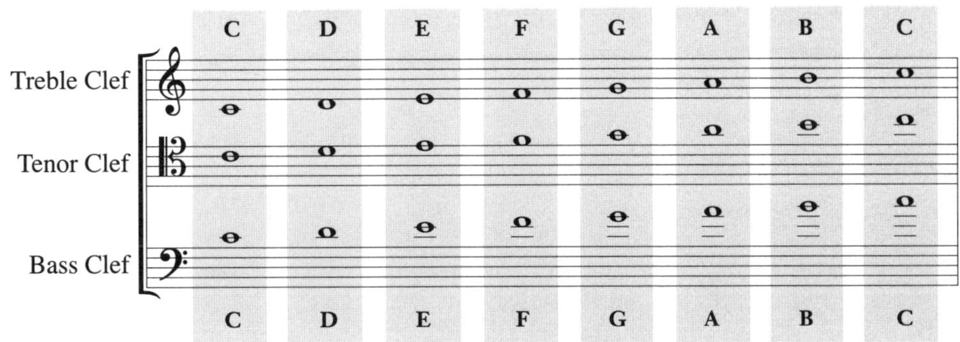


### 49. G Major Scale with Alternate Clef

*same as measures 1 and 2*

**50. Scotland's Burning**

**51. Viva la Musica**

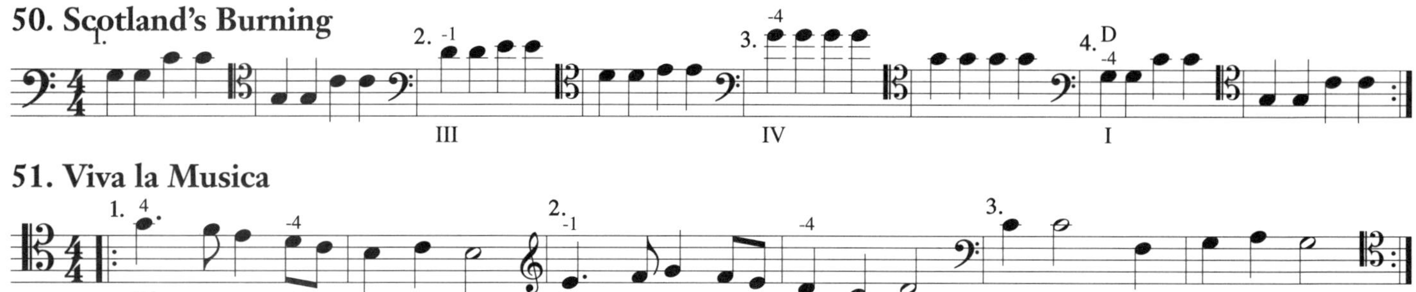

# Upper Register and Thumb Position

To reach the notes in the upper half of the fingerboard, move the thumb up onto the string no more than a whole step behind the first finger. Remember to move the bow's contact point closer to the bridge in higher positions.

**52. Upper Register Patterns**

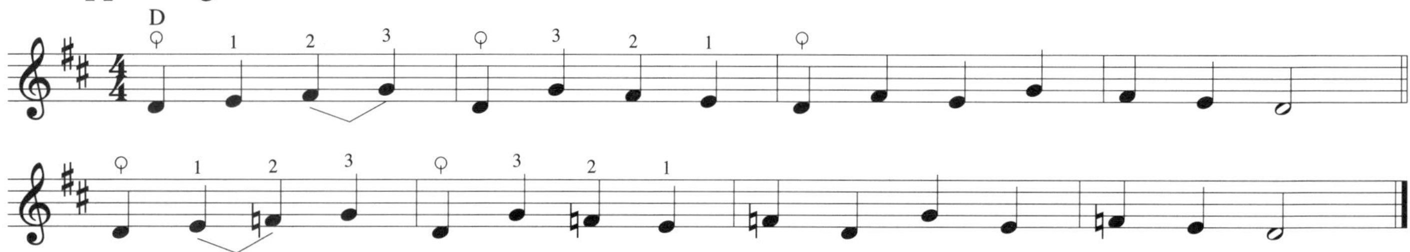

**53. A Major Scale and Arpeggio**

**54. D Major Scale and Arpeggio**

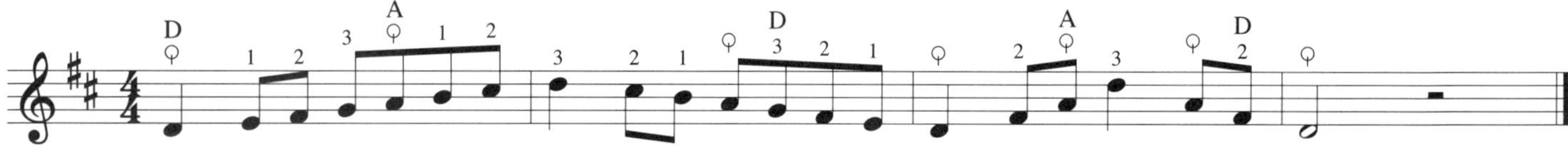

**55. D Minor Scale and Arpeggio**

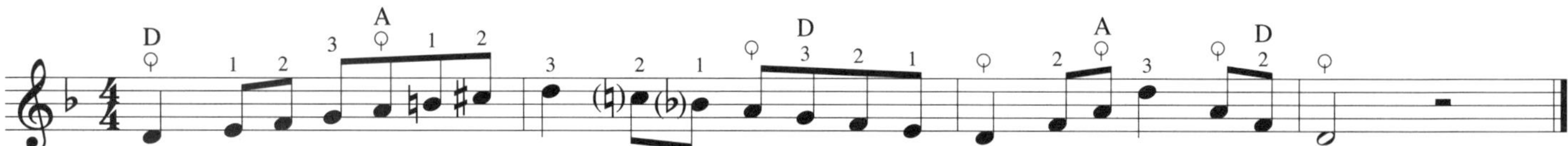

**56. E Major Scale and Arpeggio**

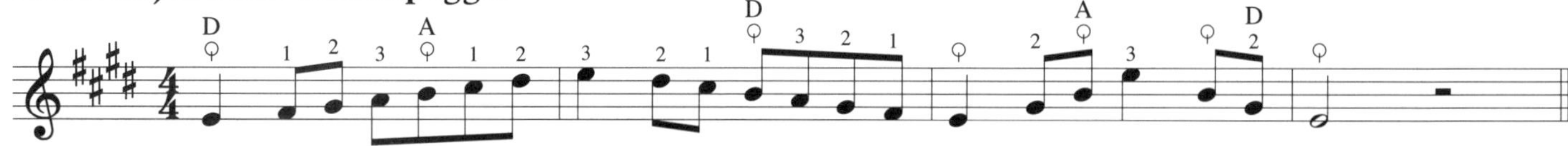

**57. C Major Scale and Arpeggio**

**58. F Major Scale and Arpeggio**

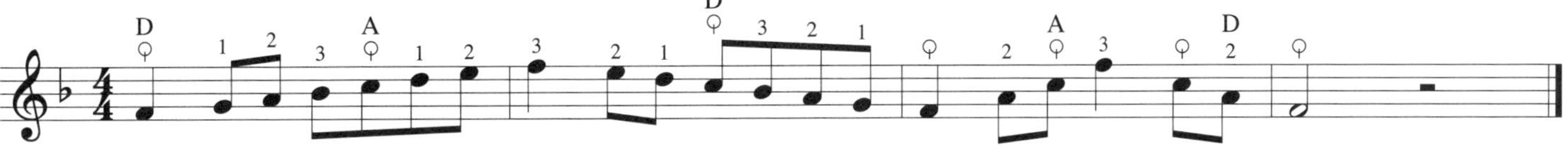


**59. Twinkle**

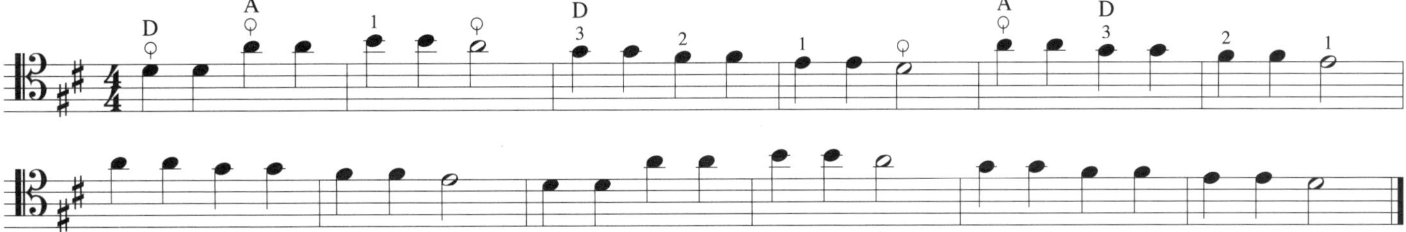


**60. Frere Jacques** (Round)

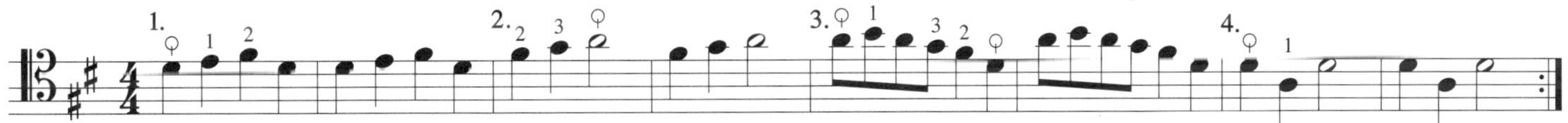


**61. Arirang**

**62. This Land Is Your Land**

**63. French Folk Song**

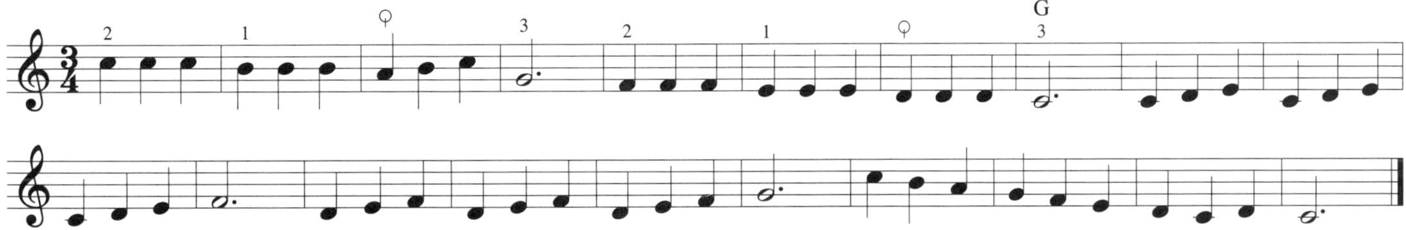


**64. Tetrachord Etude in Upper Positions**

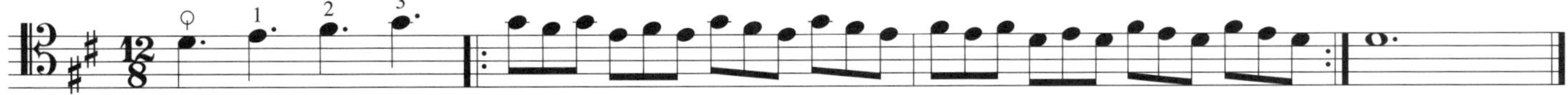

# V Scales, Arpeggios, and Thirds

Students should focus on the skills and octaves that are appropriate for their level of ability and experience. Begin learning a scale by playing each note without a pulse; listen and adjust fingertips to fine tune each pitch before moving to the next note. Then, add a pulse and learn half and quarter notes, the printed rhythm, and finally add slurs, as shown below.

Use the following checklist to guide your practice:

| | |
|---|---|
| **Tone** | ☐ Sound **projects well** with an excellent tone quality.<br>☐ **Contact point** is the correct distance between bridge and fingerboard.<br>☐ The **bow angle** is perpendicular to the string and rotated correctly.<br>☐ **Part of the bow** is correct.<br>☐ **Bow weight and speed** are balanced and produce an excellent tone that projects well. |
| **Intonation** | ☐ **Notes are consistently correct and in tune**, especially fourth and seventh scale degrees.<br>☐ **Hand placement** is correct on fingerboard, not sharp or flat.<br>☐ **Finger pattern** (half-step placement) is correct; half- and whole-step distances are correct.<br>☐ **Shifts** are clean and well-executed; **fingerings** are correct.<br>☐ **Fingertips adjust quickly**, refining the pitch after finger placement. |
| **Tempo and Rhythm** | ☐ **Tempos** are consistent; no stopping, stumbling, rushing, or dragging.<br>☐ **Rhythm** is correct.<br>☐ Exercise is **memorized** when appropriate. |

Students of different levels can learn and perform scales at the same time. Those performing more octaves should begin their scale first, as shown below.

# Major Scales, Arpeggios, and Thirds

## C Major

# G Major

Upper Octave

# D Major

# A Major

# E Major

# B Major

# F♯ Major

# F Major

100. Tuning Canon
1.
2.
3.
4.
101. Tuning Chords
102. Scales and Arpeggios - One Octave
Two Octaves
Three Octaves
103. Dominant Arpeggio
104. Thirds - Lower Octave
Upper Octave

# B♭ Major

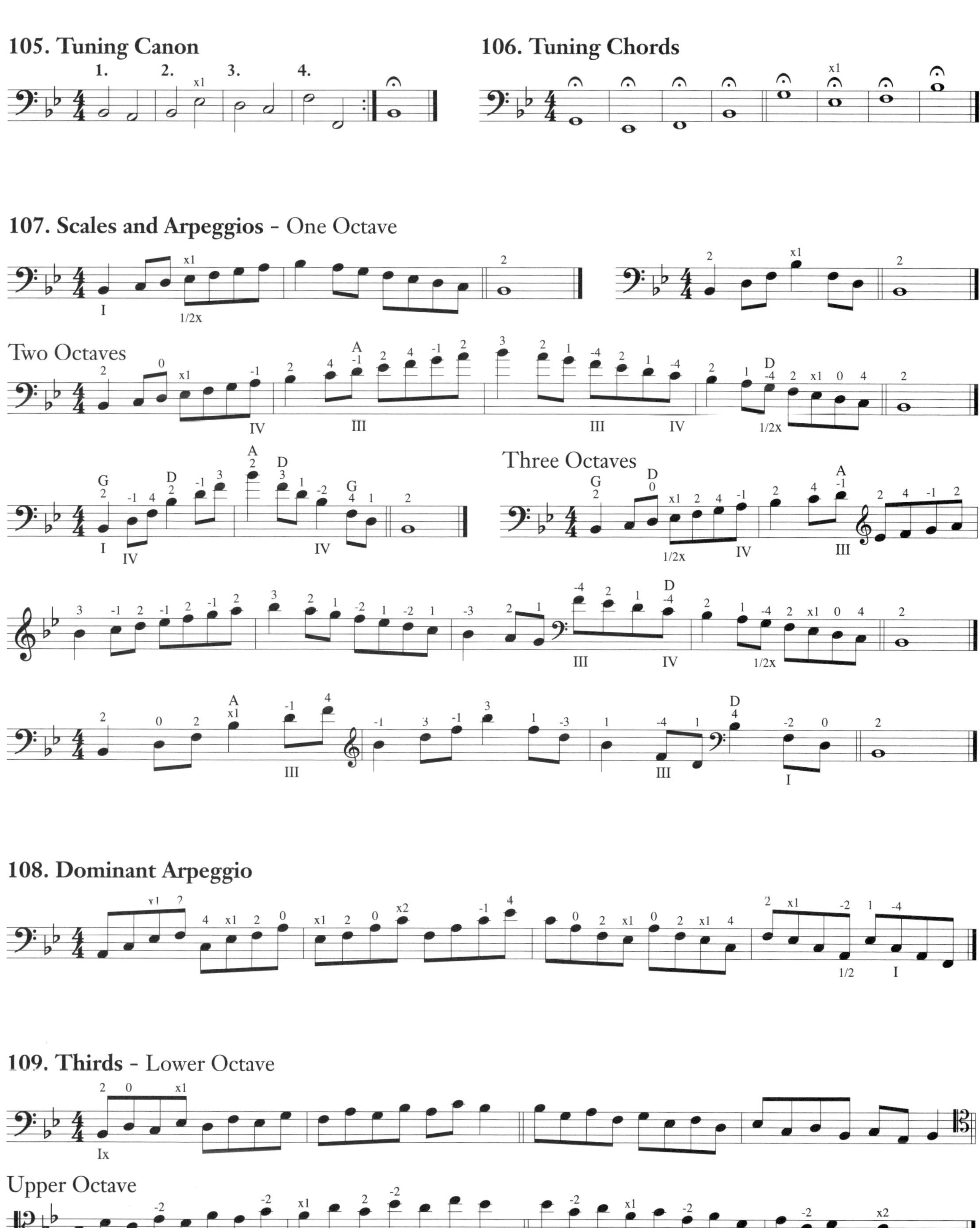

105. Tuning Canon
106. Tuning Chords
107. Scales and Arpeggios - One Octave
Two Octaves
Three Octaves
108. Dominant Arpeggio
109. Thirds - Lower Octave
Upper Octave

# E♭ Major

## 110. Tuning Canon

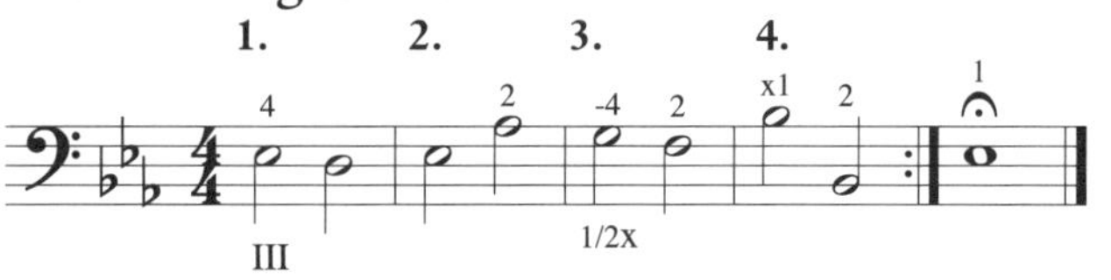

1. 2. 3. 4.

## 111. Tuning Chords

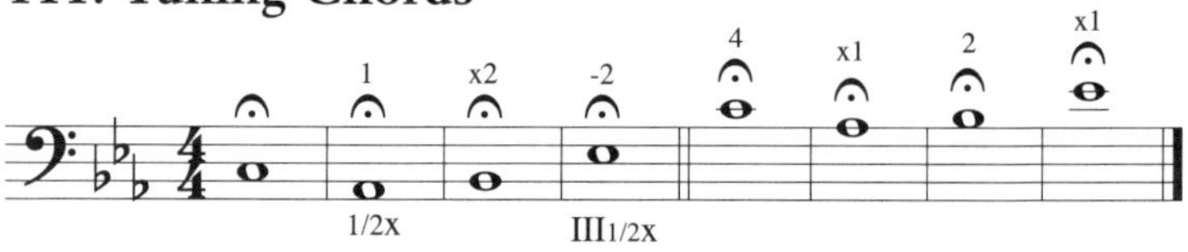

## 112. Scales and Arpeggios - One Octave

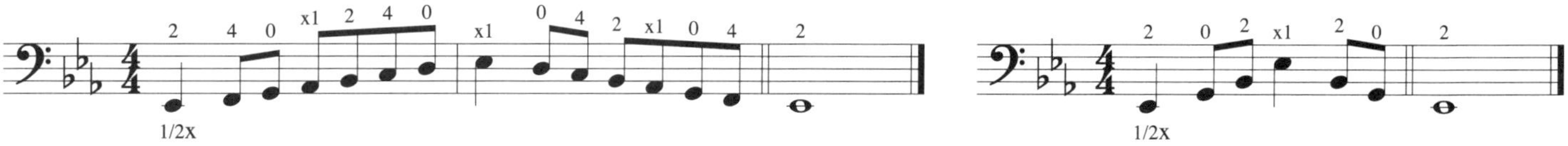

Two Octaves

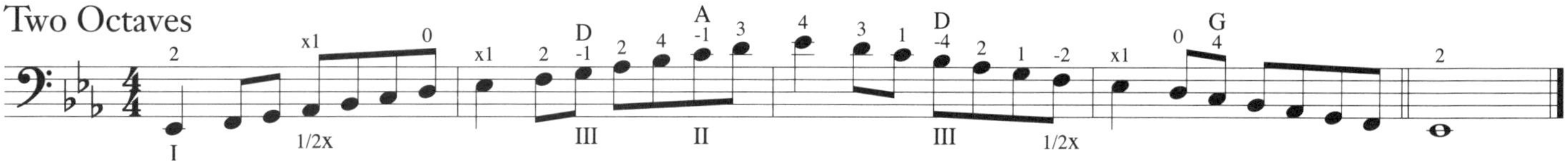

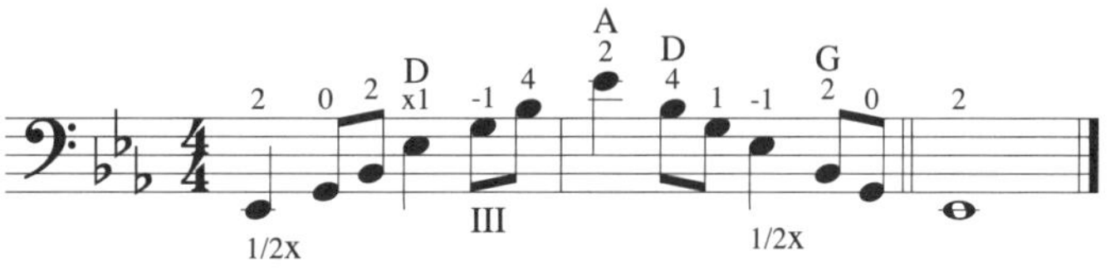

Three Octaves

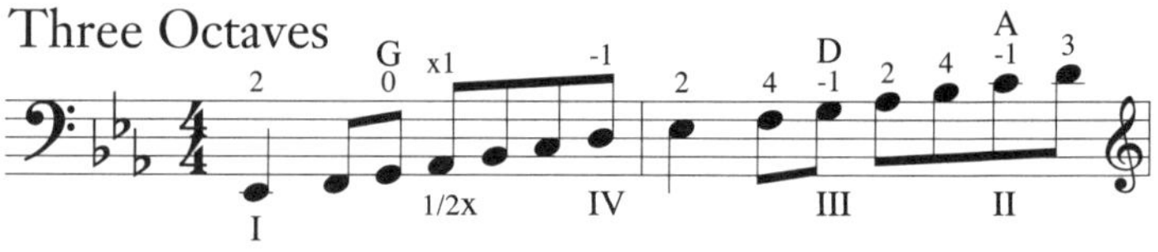

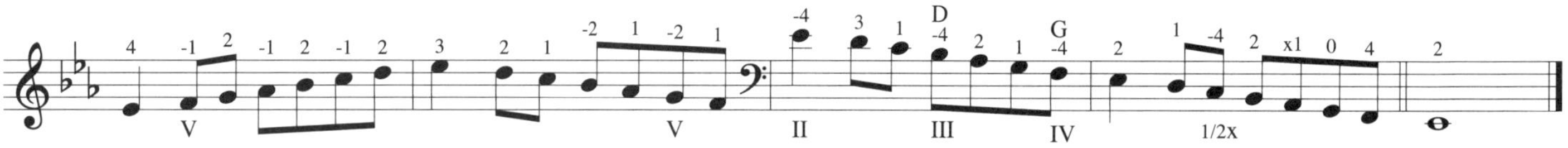

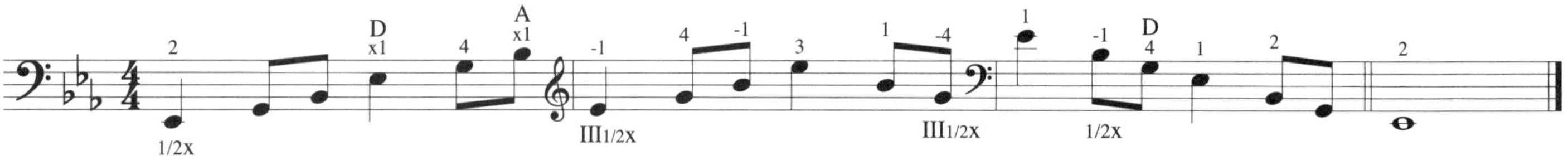

## 113. Dominant Arpeggio

## 114. Thirds - Lower Octave

# A♭ Major

# D♭ Major

# Melodic Minor Scales, Arpeggios and Thirds

## A Melodic Minor

# D Melodic Minor

# G Melodic Minor

# C Melodic Minor

# F Melodic Minor

# B♭ Melodic Minor

### 150. Tuning Canon

### 151. Tuning Chords

### 152. Scales and Arpeggios - One Octave

Two Octaves

Three Octaves

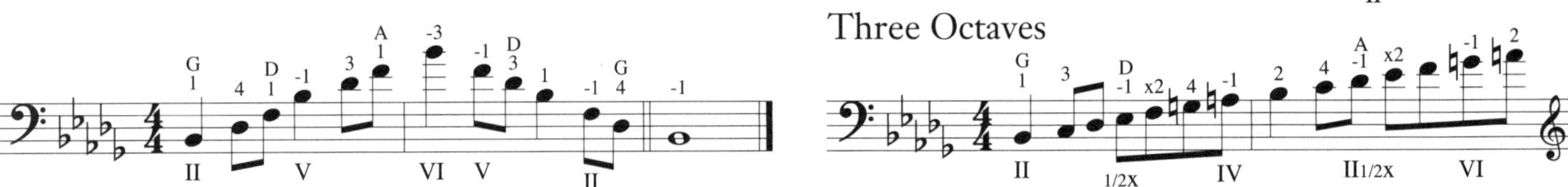

### 153. Dominant Arpeggio

### 154. Thirds - Lower Octave

Upper Octave

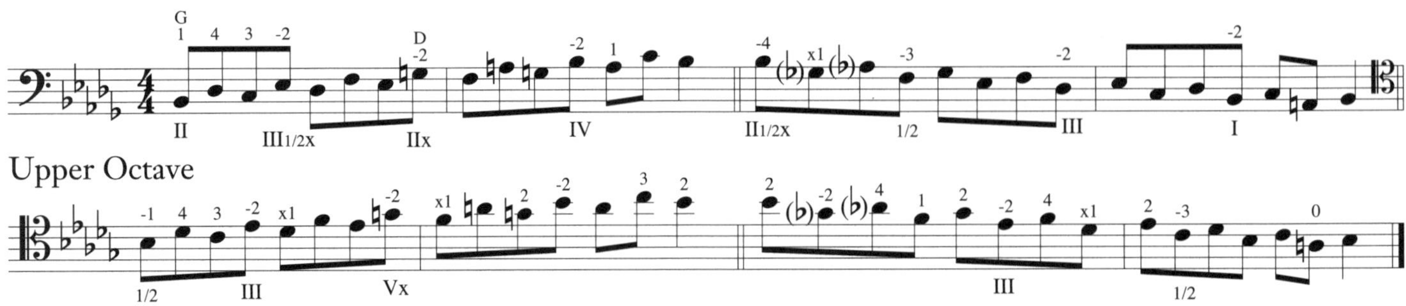

# E♭ Melodic Minor

# E Melodic Minor

# B Melodic Minor

# F♯ Melodic Minor

# C♯ Melodic Minor

# G♯ Melodic Minor

# Chromatic, Mixolydian and Blues Scales

A *chromatic* scale is made entirely of half steps.

**185. Two Octave Chromatic C Scale**

**Mixolydian and Blues Scales**

**186. B♭ Mixolydian** **Blues Scale and Arpeggio**

**187. F Mixolydian** **Blues Scale and Arpeggio**

**188. C Mixolydian** **Blues Scale and Arpeggio**

**189. G Mixolydian** **Blues Scale and Arpeggio**

**190. D Mixolydian** **Blues Scale and Arpeggio**

**191. A Mixolydian** **Blues Scale and Arpeggio**

# VI Chorales

## 192. Chorale #1

## 193. Chorale #2

## 194. Chorale #3

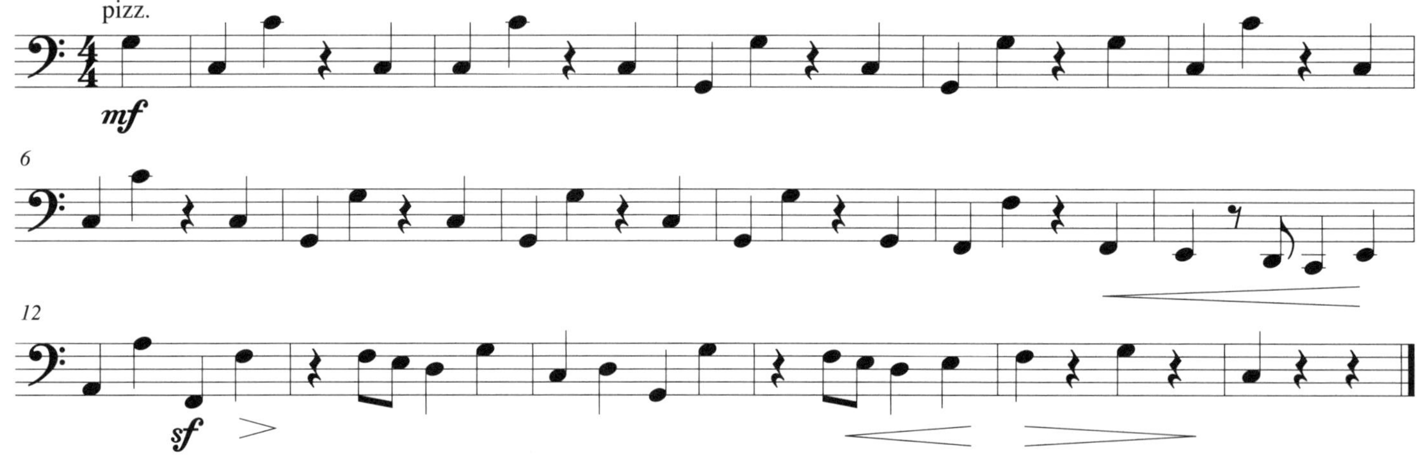


## 195. Chorale #4

## 196. Chorale #5

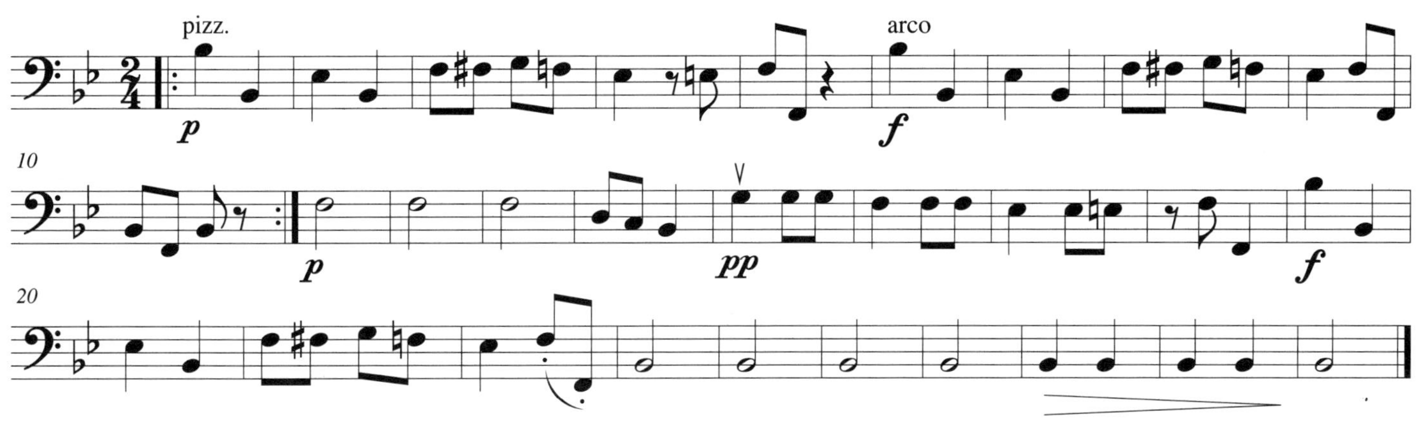


## 197. Chorale #6

## 198. Chorale #7

## 199. Chorale #8

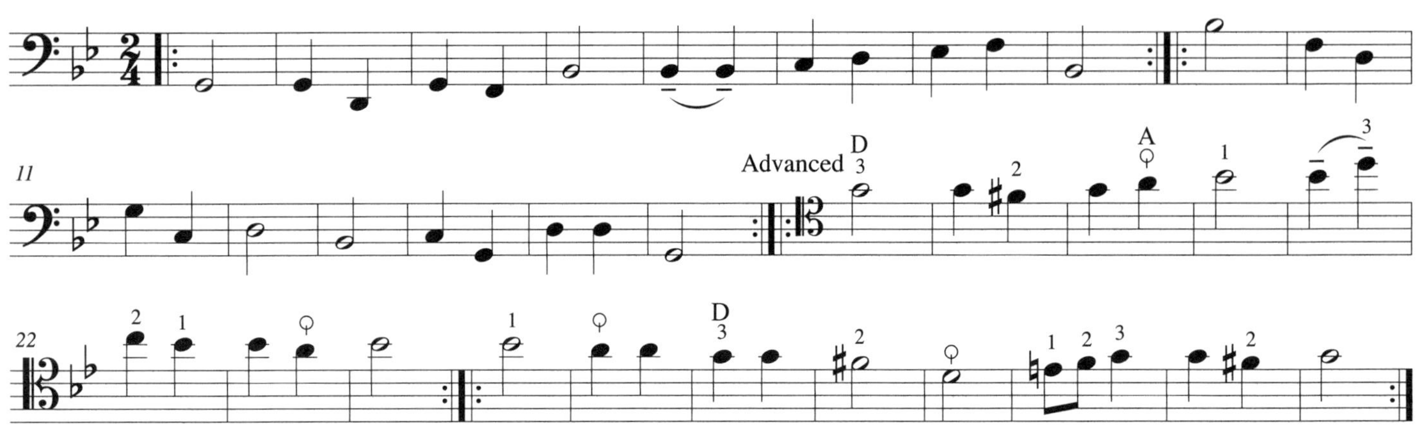


## 200. Chorale #9

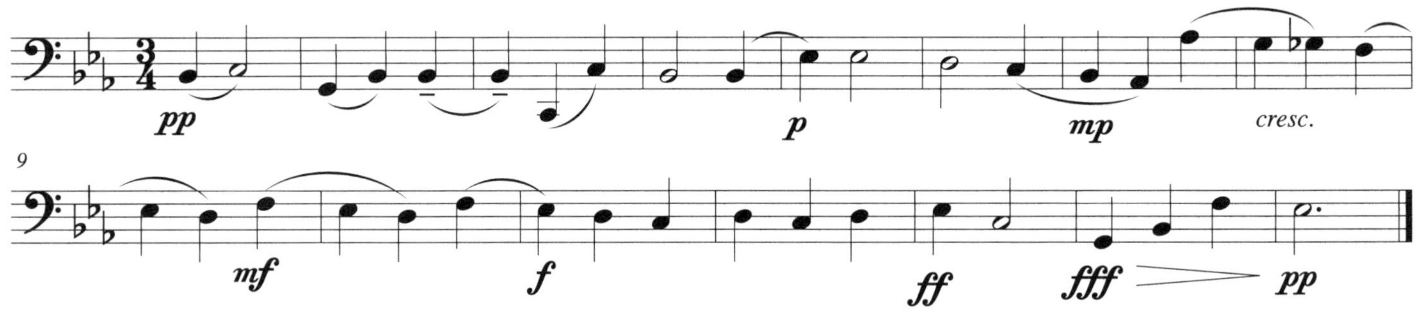


## 201. Chorale #10

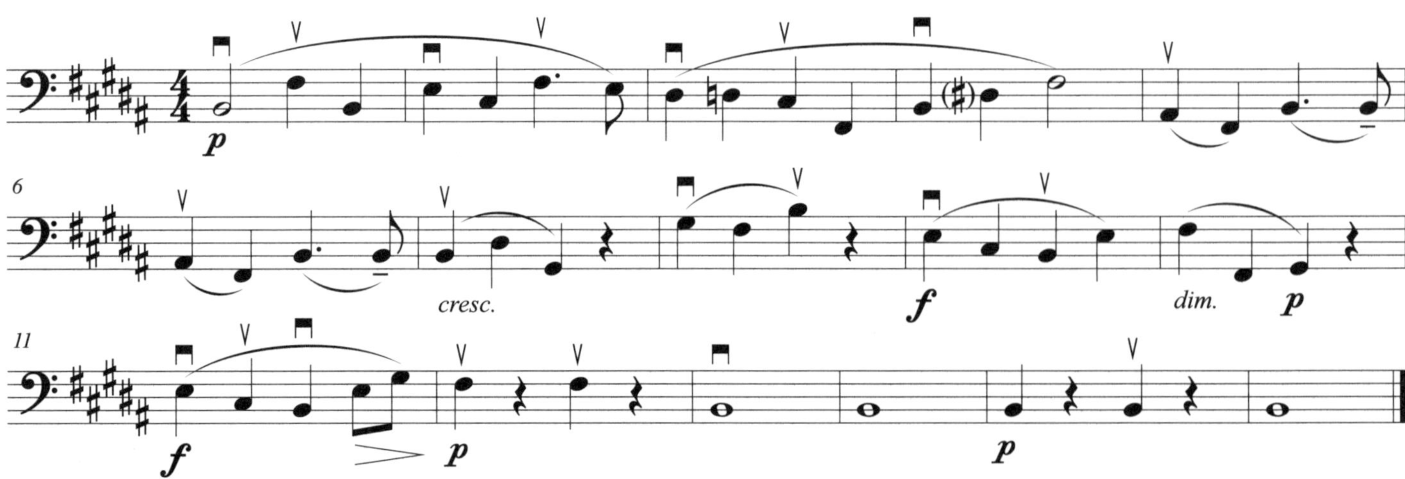

# 202. Chorale #11

# VII Rhythm Charts in a Musical Context
## A. Quarter Notes and Rests; Eighth Notes

For additional practice with quarter- and eighth-note patterns, go to Part VIII Sight Reading Exercises 260–269.

# B. Ties, Dotted Quarter Notes and Eighth Rests

For additional practice with ties, dotted quarter notes and eighth rest patterns, go to Part VIII Sight Reading Exercises 270–283.

# C. Syncopation

For additional practice with syncopated patterns, go to Part VIII Sight Reading Exercises 284–297.

# D. Intermediate Triple Meter

For additional practice with intermediate triple meter patterns, go to Part VIII Sight Reading Exercises 298–308.

# E. Triplets

For additional practice with triplet eighth-note patterns, go to Part VIII Sight Reading Exercises 309–312.

# F. Simple Sixteenth Notes

For additional practice with simple sixteenth-note patterns, go to Part VIII Sight Reading Exercises 313–324.

# G. Dotted Eighth Notes and Sixteenth Rests

For additional practice with dotted-eighth-note and sixteenth-rest patterns, go to Part VIII Sight Reading Exercises 325–334.

# H. Cut Time (¢)

**244a. and b.**

**245a. and b.**

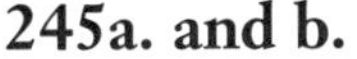

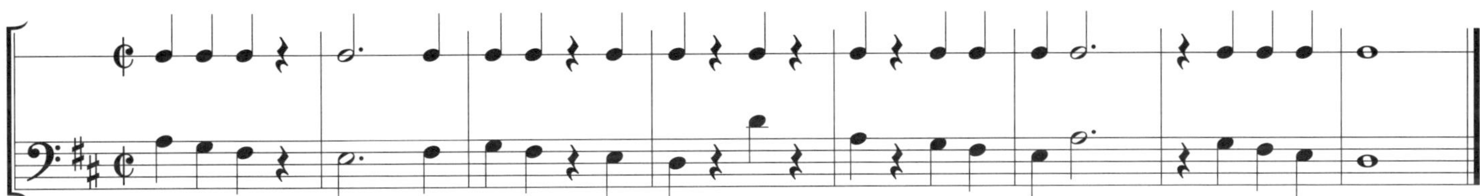

**246a. and b.**

**247a. and b.**

**248a. and b.**

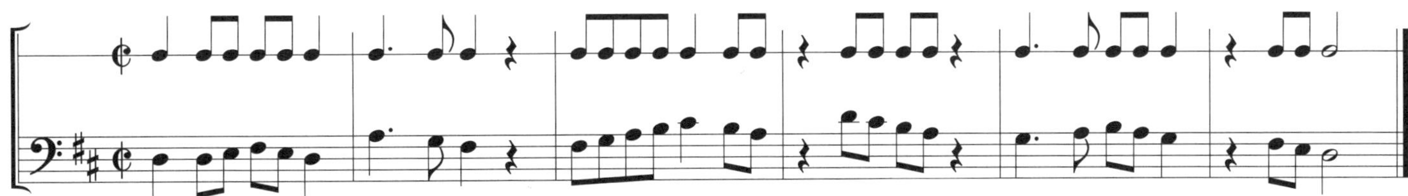

For additional practice with cut time patterns, go to Part VIII Sight Reading Exercises 335–347.

# J. Advanced Triple Meter

For additional practice with advanced triple meter patterns, go to Part VIII Sight Reading Exercises 352–369.

# K. Irregular Meter

For additional practice with irregular meter patterns, go to Part VIII Sight Reading Exercises 370–379.

# VIII Sight-Reading by Level

## A. Quarter Notes and Rests; Eighth Notes

**268.**

cresc.
p

**269.**

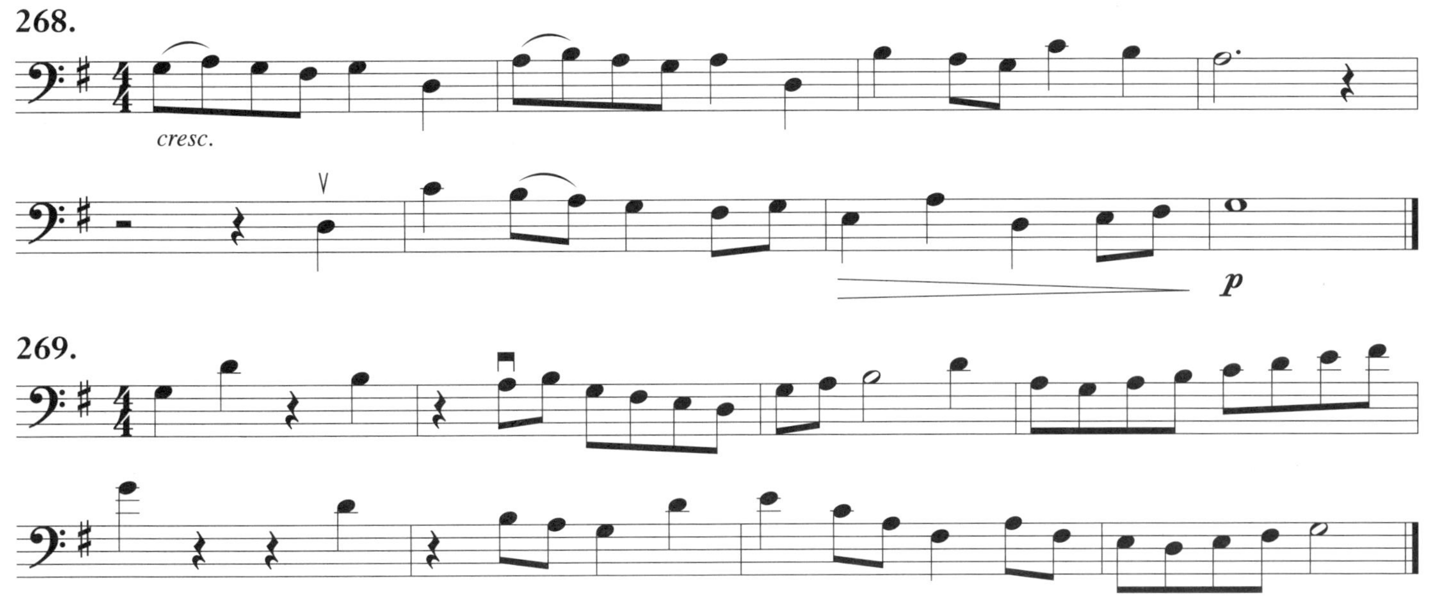

## B. Ties, Dotted Quarter Notes and Eighth Rests

**270.**

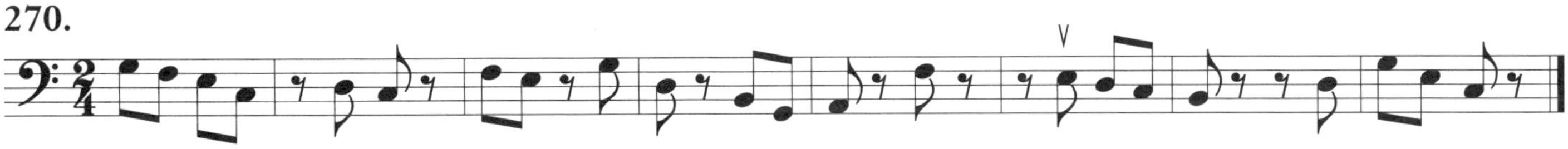

**271.**

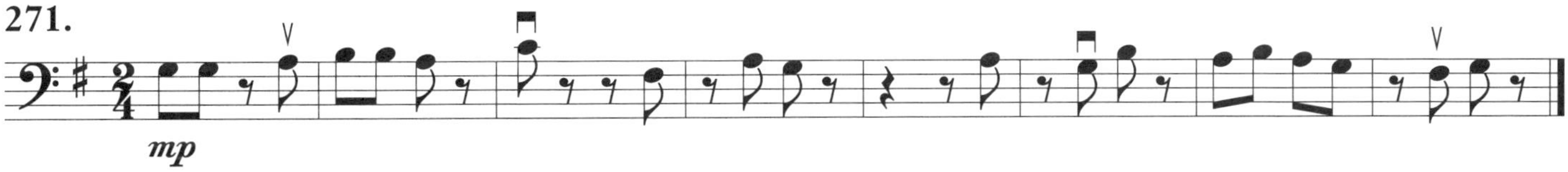
mp

**272.**

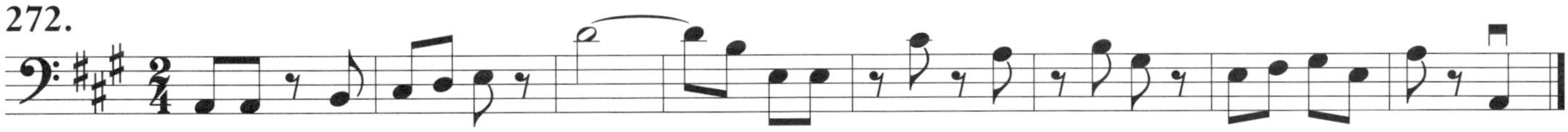

**273.**

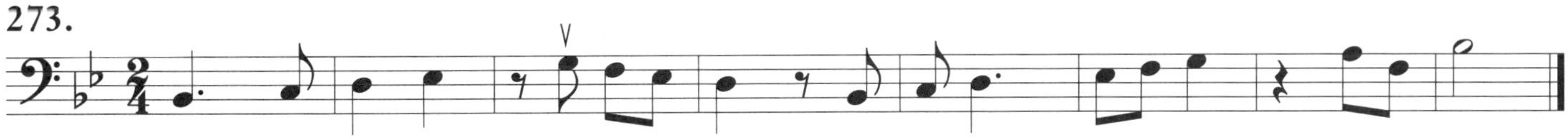

**274.**

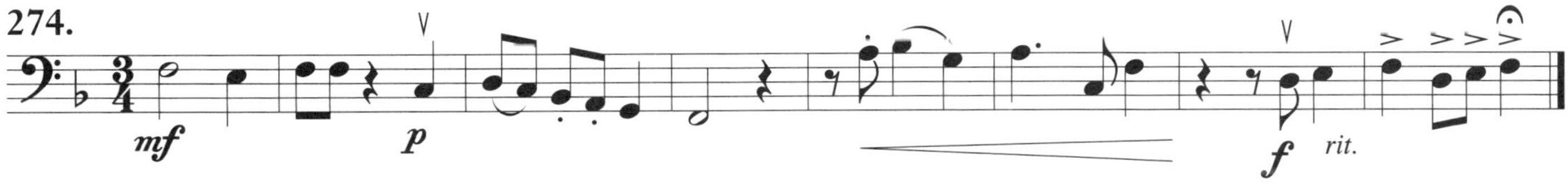
mf
p
f
rit.

**275.**

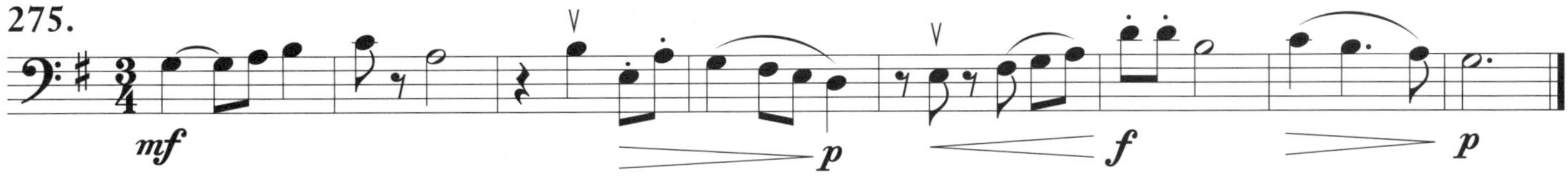
mf
p
f
p

276.
mp
f
277.
p
f
rit.
p
278.
mf
tr
f
mp
279.
mf
280.
3
mf
mp
281.
mf
f
f
p
282. Moderato
mf
rit.
283.
mf
p
f

# C. Syncopation

## D. Intermediate Triple Meter

298.

299.

300.

301.
mf
302.
mp
mf
mp
f
p
303.
304.
305.
306.
307.
308.

# E. Triplets

# F. Simple Sixteenth Notes

313.

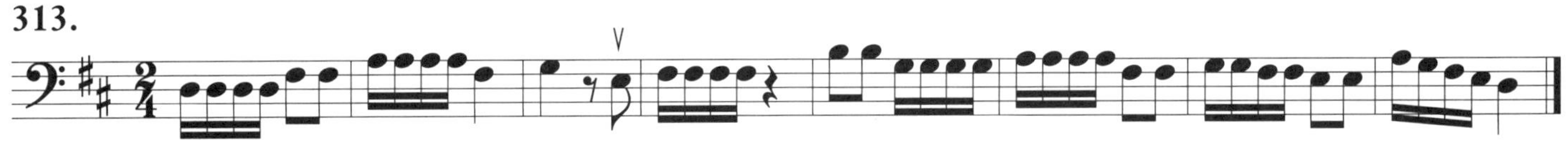

314.

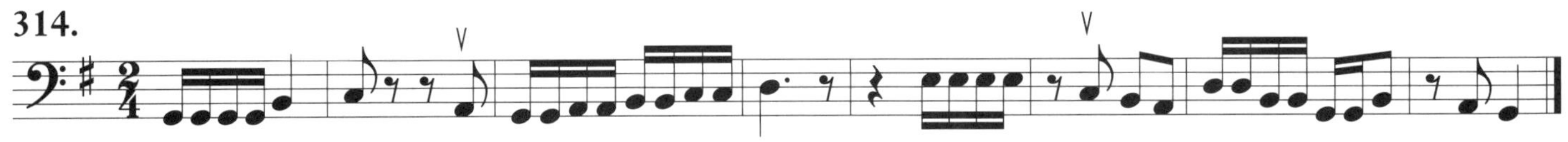

315.

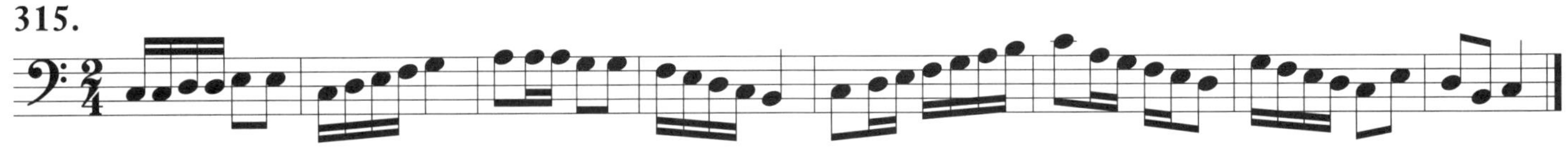

316.

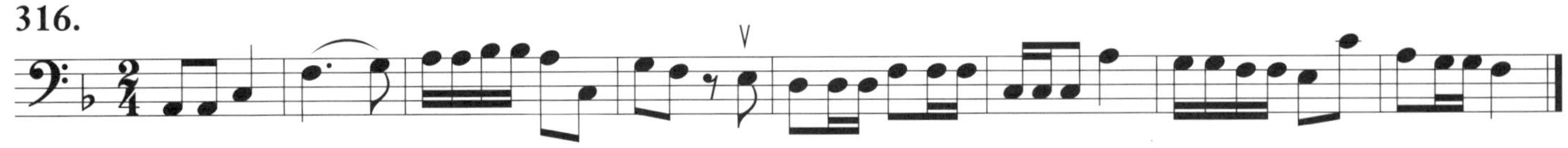

317.

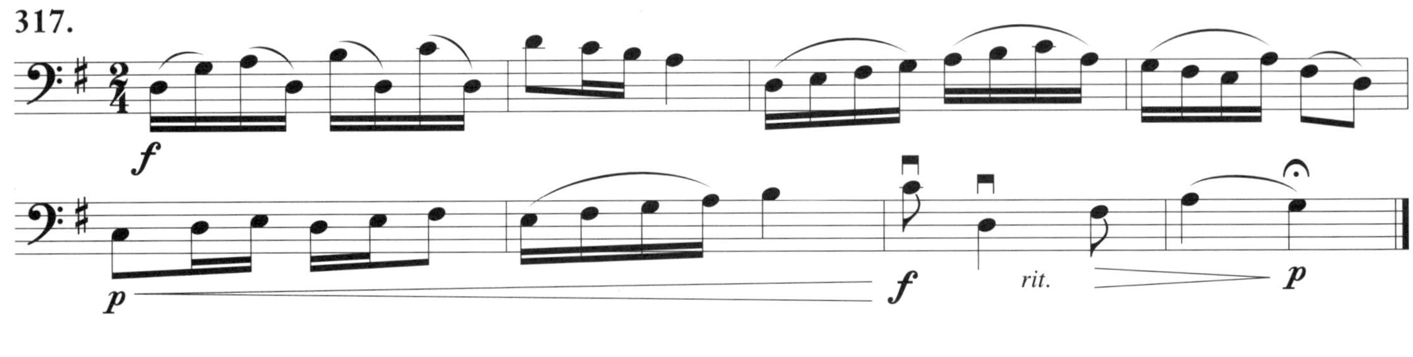

*f*

*p* *f* *rit.* *p*

318.

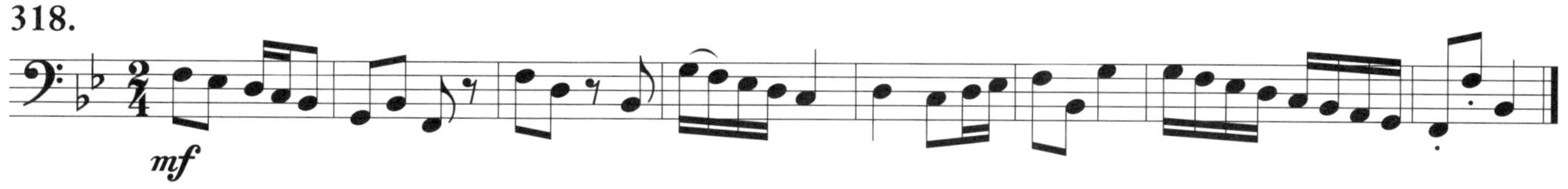

319.

320.

321.

322.

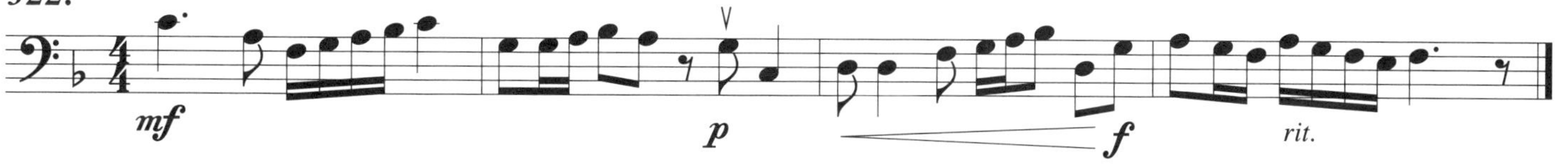

323.

324.

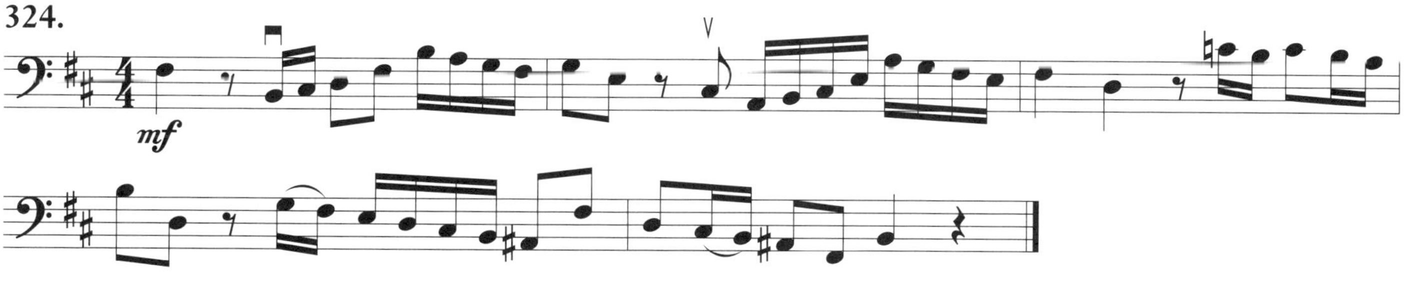

## G. Dotted Eighth Notes and Sixteenth Rests

325.

326.
p
f
mp
f
mf
rit.
327.
328.
mf
mf
rit.
329.
mp
f
mf
330.
f
p
f
p
mf
331.
Maestoso
f
3
3
332.
mf
333.
mf
p
f
rit.
334.
mf

# H. Cut Time and $\frac{3}{2}$

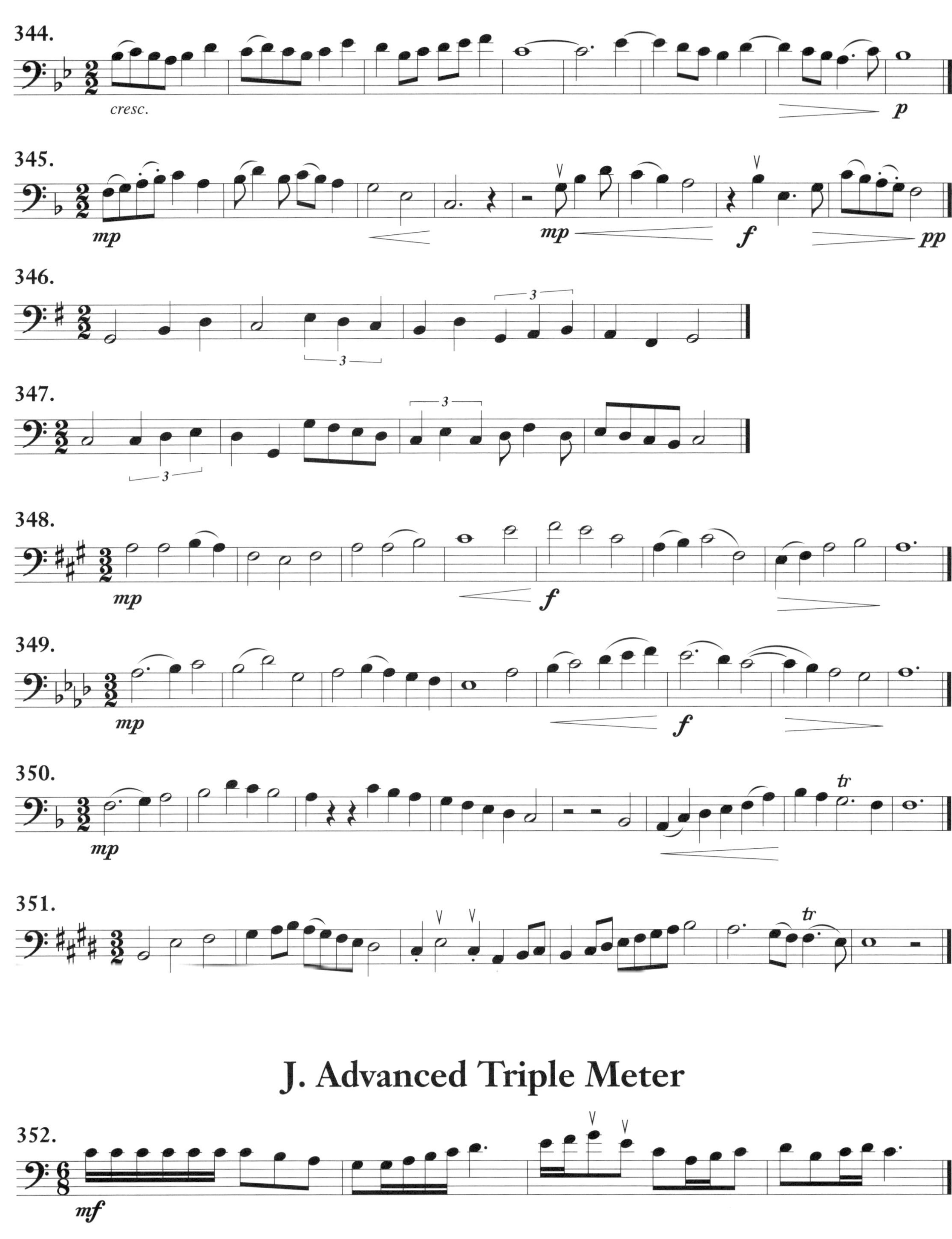


# J. Advanced Triple Meter

353.

354.
mf
rit.
355.
mf
rit.
356.
f
p
mf
rit.
357.
358.
mf
359.
360.
mf
361.
mf
f
mp

362.
363.
364.
365.
366.
367.
368.
mf
369.

# K. Irregular Meter

378.

379.

## M. Mixed Meter

380.

381.

*mf*

382.

383.

*mf*

*rit.*

384.
f
f
p
385.
mf
386.
mf
mf
N. Alternate Clefs
387.
388.
389.
mf
f
p
390.
mf
f
mp
391.
mf
f
mp

392.
mf
p
393.
mf
394.
mf
f
395.
mf
396.
mf
f